It's 1am and I can't Sleep

Jocelyn Castillo

BookLeaf Publishing

India | USA | UK

Presentation by *BookLeaf Publishing*

Web: www.bookleafpub.com

E-mail: info@bookleafpub.com

ISBN:9789358314519

First edition 2023

To my parents who always believed in me and are always there for me. I wouldn't be here without your support. I love you!

Unhinged

It was an ordinary day
Everything was quite the same
But deep down something felt strange
A feeling I can't explain
First my hands
Trembling like a leaf
Then my stomach
A pit so deep I can't see the bottom
Then my heart
Feeling like it'll leap right out my rest chest
And then the tears
Falling like gravity was their friend
So confused on what to do
I asked my brain for some clues
But everything was dark
And hectic
All at once
I couldn't think straight
And I could get rid of this weight
That stood firmly on my chest
I tried to remember what I had learned
But nothing seemed to return
As I sat on my bedroom floor
I awaited my fate
But one word suddenly stood straight

"Breathe"
One simple word
First in
And then out
My mind quieted down
My thoughts slowed down
The tremble was gone
The pit found its end
And my heart finished its race
And at that moment
I hoped I had earned some grace
Because I never wanted to do this again

Betrayal

You said you wanted to be more than Friends

But I guess you were just playing pretend

Started out friends

But didn't want it to end

You said you'd be mine

But I guess I didn't see the signs

I saw all your flaws

But didn't withdraw

You made me fall hard

And left me all scarred

You said it was all fake

And that you had made a mistake

But the fact you said that to my face

Is a feeling I can't shake

Fake Friend

I guess I'm just a bit confused

You act like you were the one that was bruised

You say hi to my family

But walk right past me.

I guess you're a good actor,

I mean you act like you never met me.

I guess I'll have to continue to wonder

If you ever stop to ponder

That what you did cut deep

The secrets I thought you would keep

We're suddenly sprawled out so everyone could
see

I guess I just have to understand

That the past is gone

And the present moves on

I'll keep our memories safe

And watch who you once were fade away

The Best Friend

You tell me, he's a good guy
He's kind and sweet
I'm happy for you
But it's still cuts deep
Don't get me wrong
You deserve to be happy
And I am happy for you
But there's a part of me
That feels like I'll never catch up.
It feels like I'm destined to be alone
While you live happily ever after
You talk about his bright eyes
And I can't find one that I'll look into mine
You say he opens the door
And I continue to open my own
You say he buys you flowers
And mine have never bloomed
But how is this something you explain
The thing is you don't
You sit and listen
And smile and laugh
And be the best friend you can be
Cause what matters is that they're happy
Right?

Fake News

I keep trying to forget you
But I just can't seem to
I think I see you everywhere
Yet you don't care what I do.
But the worst is yet to come
Cause I'm already too far gone.
It's already too late,
To save me from my fate
Because the bad news are this,
I fell for you,
And in the end
It was all fake
And made up in my head

Happy Single

I say I'm happy single
Which is usually true
But there are times
I wouldn't mind
Having a hand to hold
Someone to open the door
A jacket when it's cold
Someone to call when I'm down
Someone who gives me butterflies with just one
look
Someone to just be mine
But I'm happily single
As you can obviously see
But I don't know
It's nice to sometimes just daydream

Unrequited Love

My heart, an open book, laid bare and true,
But your feelings didn't mirror the view.
I danced in dreams where your name did gleam,
While you wandered in a different dream.
With each unspoken word and silent plea,
I hoped you'd see me
With a gleam in your eye
But the story of love always has a different
ending
We each played our part
but we'll forever be apart
I hope one day the story ends,
with a love that will always remain.

Strangers Now

In friendship's warm embrace
we once did dwell.
Laughter and tears
Filled our days
But even the closest of friends
Can silently drift away

A friendship so vibrant
It could light up the night
Is now so dark
There's nothing in sight

Out story ended too soon
Too many pages left unread
Too many pages left unturned
And we'll never the end

And even though we drifted apart
And time moves on
The memories will never change
Time will stand still
And I'll remember when we were the best of
friends

Self-Love

In the mirrors gaze,
I see a precious gem
In fact she's my very best-friend
she's beautiful
Smart
Funny
Confident
Pretty
And that's just the start.
I embraced who I am
And fell in love
And you should too
So embrace who you are
And cherish your worth
For there's no one like you on this earth
So be kind to you
And smile each day
Knowing you're uniquely you.

Unattainable

12

I knew I had to let you go
For I only would suffer more
Holding on to what could've been
Instead I'll hold on to this dream in my head
And watch as you fall in love with someone else

Mom and Dad

With each passing day
I notice a change
That once brown hair is now gray
The aches and pains are here to stay
And think about your age
And that you won't be able to forever stay
I really don't want you to go
But unfortunately, youth does fade
so I'll cherish every moment
For I don't know the day,
Everything will change
And my life will never be the same

Behind closed doors

I smile for all to see
But the struggle within hurts deep
How long can I keep this up
Without giving up
The mask is getting uncomfortable
The more tears it blocks,
The harder it is to see
The more screams it mutes,
The louder the ringing gets in my ears
The mask is making everyone happy.
But causing my downfall
What do you think?

I miss you

15

They say I dodged a bullet
And I should be glad
That you left
And I stayed behind
But the memories come rushing back
I try to push them aside
And tell everyone I'm fine
But every night,
When the darkness creeps in
And sleep overtakes me
Your face is the last I see
And I wonder if you also see me

The Girl Who Reads

I flip a page and the story begins
The story starts with a girl who is shy
Doesn't want love
And is scared to even try
Next, we meet the boy
Everyone seems to like
But who's really lonely inside
In every line, I find a cherished place.
Living through the characters, their highs and
lows,
The girl and the boy fall in love
And live happily ever after.
And, suddenly I am back to where I was.
No longer in this world full of love,
But in a world where love is hard to find.
I wish life was a book.
Where love doesn't hurt
And your heart doesn't get broken
And every story had a happy ending

Hopeless Romantic

They find beauty in sunsets, in rainbows, and
stars,
In the way two souls connect, from near or afar.
For a hopeless romantic, love's a grand art,
A masterpiece painted on the canvas of the
heart.

The Day You Left

The day you left me
Was the day the world lost its color
And the sun hid away
I wish I could go back
And give you one more embrace.
One that would last forever
So that you could never leave
and so that we could just be
So that when you took your last breath
your last memory would be of you with me

To My Best Friend

19

Dear best friend,
I love you to death
Through thick and thin,
we've laughed and cried.
With you everything is clear
and I'm glad you're by my side
As we go through each year
I hope we always stay close
Because you're my soulmate
in sister form.

The Tears on My Pillow

20

The tears on my pillow,
know more about my tearful nights
than my closest friends.
They know about the pain, I hide within
They know, but won't tell a soul
Which is why I trust them more.